Last name............................
First name............................
Adress............................
Tel............................
Name school............................

A a

alien

B b

boat

C c

castle

D d

dinosaur

Ee

elephant

Ff

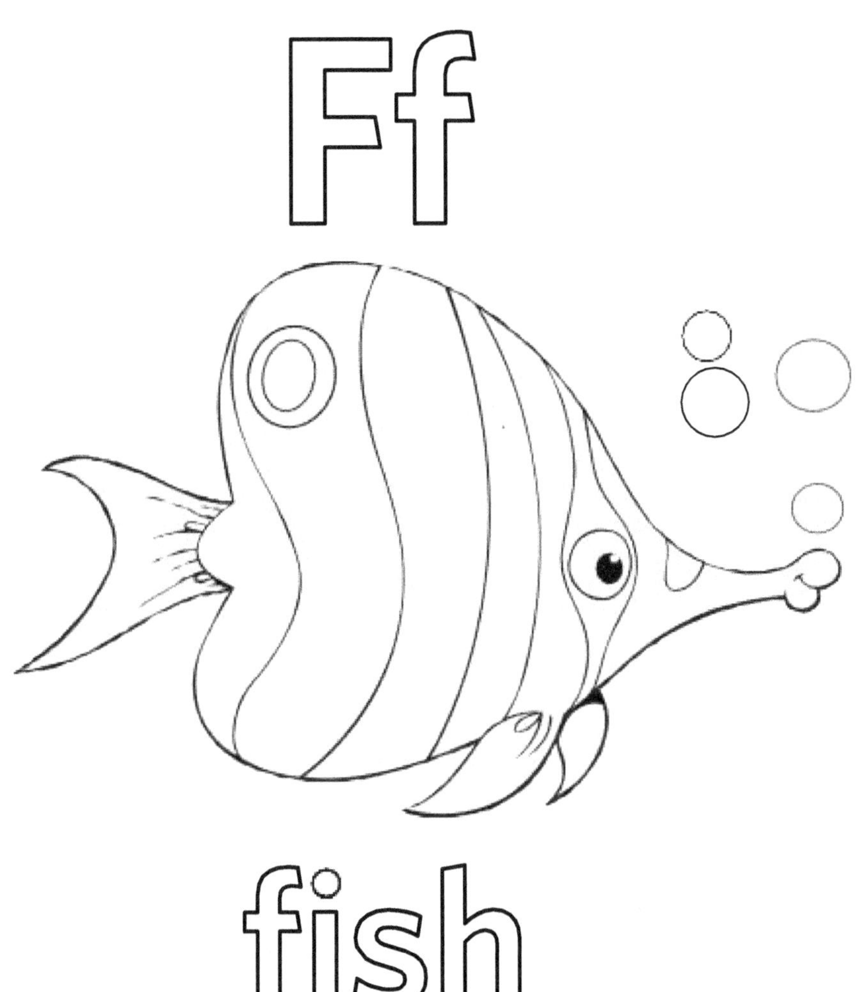

fish

Gg

guitar

Hh

helicopter

Ii

insect

Jj

jungle

Kk

kangaroo

Ll

lion

Mm

monkey

Nn

nurse

Oo

octopus

Pp

parrot

Qq

queen

Rr

rocket

Ss

spider

Tt

train

Uu

umbrella

Vv

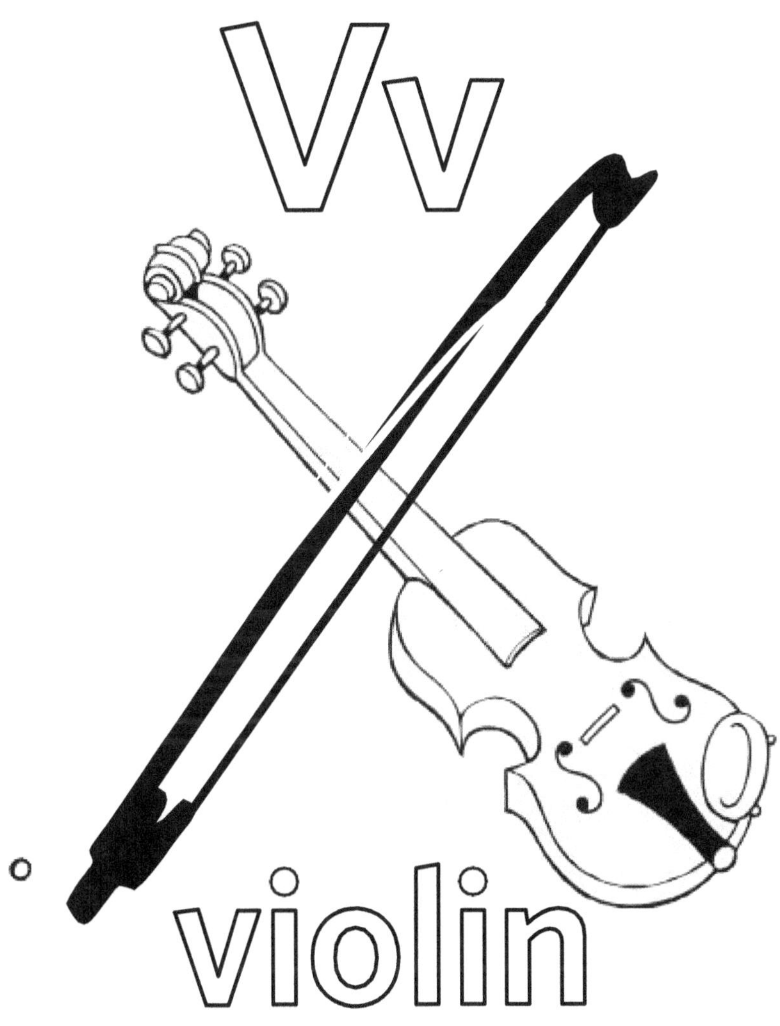

violin

Ww

whale

Xx

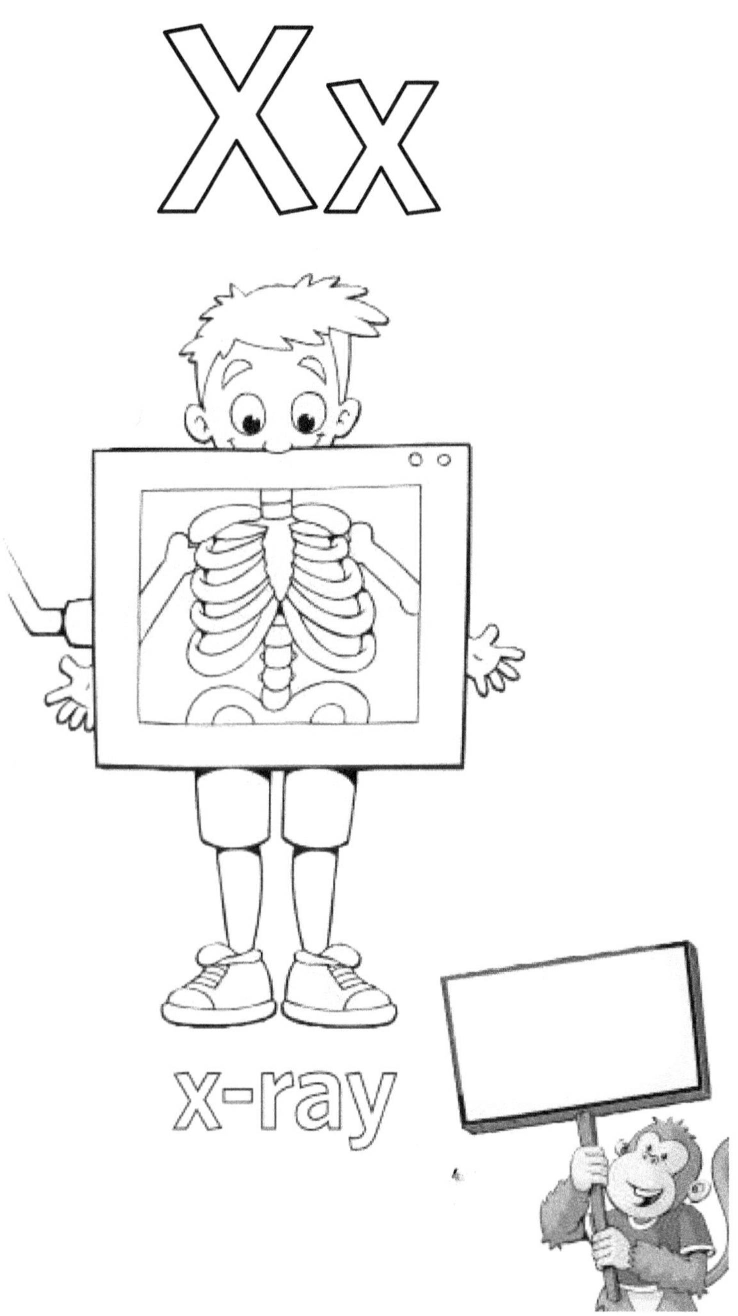

x-ray

Yy

young

Zz

ZOO

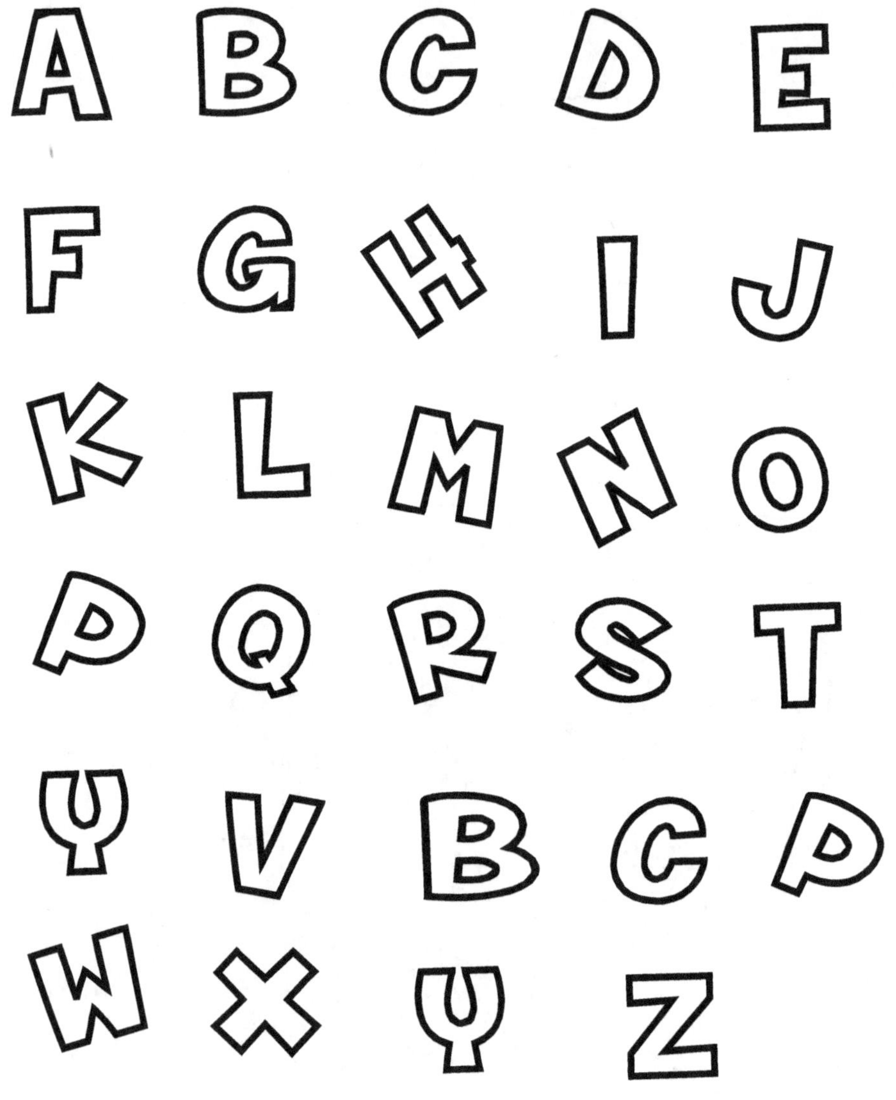

draw

draw

draw

www.ingramcontent.com/pod-product-compliance
Lightning Source LLC
Chambersburg PA
CBHW052137150726
48002CB00006B/2648